A Child Was Chosen

A Child Was Chosen

by Julia Pierce

Wesley Press
Indianapolis, Indiana

Cover Design and Illustrations by
Ken Raney

© Copyright 1984 by Wesley Press
All Rights Reserved
Published by Wesley Press
Indianapolis, IN 46250
Printed in the United States of America
ISBN: 0-89827-023-5

Table of Contents

	Page
Acknowledgments	7
Chapter 1 - Only One Young Man	9
Chapter 2 - Off to Fairmount Bible School .	13
Chapter 3 - Has God been talking to you about Africa?	17
Chapter 4 - We're Home	21
Chapter 5 - Lots of Love	27
Chapter 6 - No Repeat Performance	31
Chapter 7 - Two of Everything	35
Chapter 8 - Confident in Their Trust	41
Chapter 9 - Separating the Sheep and Goats	45
Chapter 10 - Elephant Hunting	49
Chapter 11 - A Broken Heart	55
Chapter 12 - No Passage Out	59
Chapter 13 - God's Design for Frank and Zola	63
Chapter 14 - God's Design for Marion	65
Chapter 15 - God's Design for Marilyn	69
Chapter 16 - God's Design for Larry	75

Acknowledgments

Sincere thanks is given to Dr. Marilyn Birch and Rev. Marion Birch who provided much of the information for this book and checked the manuscript for accuracy. Thanks is given to Dr. Larry Birch for sending information on his life. The information has been supplemented with facts researched from *The Wesleyan Missionary*, 1919 - 1940. Appreciation is expressed to the archives of The Wesleyan Church, Marion, Indiana, for access to these copies.

Chapter 1
Only One Young Man

"Mornin, Reverend."

The minister looked up as he continued to pull at the stubborn tent stake. "Good morning, John. How are you feeling today?"

"Much better, thank you," he replied slipping down off his horse. "Let me give you a hand there."

Together the two men tugged and wiggled the stake.

"Sorry you missed our last service," the minister said regretfully. "I believe the evangelist preached better last night than any of the other nights during this revival meeting."

"I'm sorry I couldn't be there. Say, Gertrude told me someone went forward to be saved."

"Yep, young Frank Birch got saved last night."

"Was he the only one?" inquired John.

"Yep," the minister confirmed.

"Only one young man . . ." John's words drifted and got lost in the racket of the tent falling.

Being 16, the oldest of nine children, and the only boy for several years, many of the home responsibilities fell to Frank. He helped his father in the fields, fed and watered the farm animals, cut firewood, watched the younger children, and pumped and carried water for what seemed to be bottomless tubs when it was laundry day or time for Saturday evening baths. Frank was a sensitive young man and wanted to please his parents.

Night after night he had attended the special tent services with his family. He sat up straight on the backless benches and listened carefully although he was so miserable inside that his thoughts drifted as he struggled with the decision he must make.

He thought, "I know I have sinned. . . ."

"I want to ask forgiveness so Jesus will be my Lord, but I'm afraid He'll ask me to leave home and go to Bible school. . . ."

"No one else is going forward. . . ."

"Why is my heart pounding so hard? . . ."

"I wish this service was over and we were home. . . ."

It was a hard decision for Frank to make. He struggled with it night and day during the six weeks of revival services. He knew that God was asking for his entire life — not just his heart. He felt God was asking him to attend Bible school and prepare for the ministry.

His thoughts ran uncontrolled, "If I accept Jesus, I'll want to go to Bible school. . . ."

"I must stay home to help. Dad isn't well and Mother will need me to help. . . ."

"I must decide what to do. . . ."

"Oh, Lord, please help me. . . ."

Frank prayed and prayed. He spent many hours out in the woods and in the hayloft torn between his desire to follow Jesus and his family obligations. Each revival service magnified his misery and need.

These services had been each evening for six weeks and no one had accepted Jesus. God had put a burden on the minister and people not to close the meeting. On the very last evening, Frank made a decision to follow Jesus. His heart was pounding so hard during the service that he looked around to be sure no one else could hear it. He squirmed and fidgeted through the songs and message. He thought his heart would leap out of his body when they stood for the altar call. Without hesitation and with great relief, Frank went forward.

Frank Birch was only one young man, but God had a special plan for his life. No one, but God, knew what results would be accomplished because one young man listened to God's call and obeyed.

Chapter 2
Off to Fairmount Bible School

Much prayer was given before Frank approached his parents about Bible school. His parents believed in the British tradition of giving one son to the military, one son to the clergy, and one son to help at home. It would have been only natural for them to expect Frank to stay on the farm while his brothers and sisters were being raised. He had been so good to help through the previous years.

Frank's parents moved to Solon Center, Michigan, when only log cabins were available. Later they ordered a partially assembled house from Sears, Roebuck, and Company. Frank and his father rode on the wagon to pick up the lumber from the railroad. Long hours of hard work, frustration, tears, and joy were shared as they built the large farm house.

All 12 grades of school were held in a one-room schoolhouse and taught by one teacher. One of Frank's biggest jobs was to help the younger family members get ready each morning. Making sure each one was washed, teeth brushed, dressed, and needed assignments in hand was no easy chore.

Recreation on the farm had to be made since none was provided for them. They never had television, skateboards, mopeds, or computers. They invented their own fun. Bobsledding was one of their favorite winter pastimes. As many children as possible would pile on a sled. As they raced down the hill, they would try to throw each other off before reaching the bottom. You would think that the long journey back up the hill would drain every drop of energy, but it wasn't long before they were piled high and off again.

Hunting was another favorite pastime for Frank. He had learned at an early age how to properly use a rifle and get small game. Being a very good shooter, Frank would wait until there were enough water snakes sunning on the fence and then pop them off in quick succession.

Frank's heart was torn between his love for his family and his love for God. How could he ask permission to leave home when they needed him so much?

"Dad, could we talk?" inquired Frank.

"Sure, son. Have a seat while I finish milking," insisted his father.

"Dad, I've been praying about something," Frank hesitated.

"I know," assured his father. "I've noticed you head for the woods and hayloft quite a bit lately. What have you been praying about?"

"I believe God wants me to go to Bible school, Dad."

"Bible school . . . Are you sure that is what God wants for you?" asked his father.

"I'm sure, Dad. I've prayed about it for weeks and God will not release me from it. I don't want to hurt you and Mom. Please pray about it," encouraged Frank.

"We have been, Son. Your Mom and I have

known that God has been talking to you. We weren't sure what He was saying, but we want God's best for you. Going to Bible school won't be easy for you or us. You will have to work and study hard. We will help in anyway that we can."

Frank's heart leaped for joy. The heaviness was gone. He would soon be headed for Fairmount Bible Training School outside Fairmount, Indiana. (This school was located on the campground of the Indiana Conference of the Wesleyan Methodist Church. It was later moved to Marion, Indiana.)

There were many things to do before school started. The fee for tuition would have to be saved. Clothing would have to be made. Frank would need a job. The list went on and on.

The day of departure came quickly and yet seemed to be so distant. It would be hard to say good-bye, and yet, Frank was so excited about his new life ahead. He was anxious to begin. Father and Mother wanted to help Frank. They had little money but never lacked in giving their love and encouragement.

Frank found Bible school very enjoyable. He was one of about 30 students. He studied hard to become a minister. To help pay his expenses, he got up at 4:00 a.m. to clean a dentist office and a factory. His family also sent in produce, potatoes, and beans to assist the school.

Zola Kinnison arrived at Fairmount Bible Training School at the beginning of Frank's second year. She had overheard some of the girls mentioning Frank and wanted to meet this young man. The school rules and one's upbringing would not have permitted her or him to just go up and say, "Hi!" They would have to meet each other through another person. They weren't to hold hands or even talk between classes. If they wanted to leave the grounds or have a date, they would have to be chaperoned.

Zola and Frank's friendship blossomed as they spent more time together. Frank was interested in courting Zola but needed a horse and buggy. With a lot of flattery and talking, he got his Father to buy a new horse. Prince was a good horse and came in handy when Frank wished to take Zola for a ride.

Chapter 3

Has God been talking to you about Africa?

It wasn't long before Frank was thinking about asking Zola to marry him. The family would have to meet her first. Thoughtfully he made plans to take Zola home during a school vacation. She was nervous about meeting his family and talked all the way. Frank's family was also nervous and scared about meeting her.

"What if she doesn't like us?" inquired one.

"Stand still, Margaret," insisted Mother tying her bow. "Of course, she'll like you."

"Is she pretty?" asked David.

"I'm sure she is," replied Mother. "Now everyone stand still and let me look at you. Gertrude, you'll have to wash your hands again."

"But, Mother. . . ."

"Move, young lady," said Mother as she gave her a light swat.

"Why do we have to dress up?"

"To make a good impression on Zola," replied Mother. "We don't want to scare her to death."

"Now how could we scare her?" questioned Dad as he viewed the children. "We have a very good-looking family, and they are going to be angels while Zola is here. Right, children?"

"Yes, sir," answered the eight children together.

"Here they come," shouted one excitedly.

"Oh . . . she's pretty!"

Zola was given a warm welcome and soon was loved as a member of the family. It took a few tries before she could name all seven sisters without twisting their names up, but she learned quickly.

Frank and Zola were married and took their first pastorate at Solon Center, Michigan. They loved the church and community people. It wasn't unusual to find them doing acts of kindness for others. Willingly they shared whatever they had. Sometimes it was a pie, a word of encouragement, time to stay with a sick person, a helping hand when needed or a cheery smile and a wave. People loved to be with them.

Frank and Zola had pastored almost a year when God began talking to them about missionary service. One morning following their individual devotional times, Frank decided to mention it.

"Zola, has God been saying anything to you about missionary service in Africa?" asked Frank.

"Yes, I think He has, but I figured if He was talking to me about that, He would also be saying something to you."

"For several times during my devotions I have seen myself standing under a palm tree. I was wearing a Safari suit and pith helmet. I had a Bible in my hand and was preaching to some Africans."

"What do you think it means?" questioned Zola.

"Probably nothing, but I'm not sure. We have so much to do for God here. He couldn't be asking us to go to Africa."

"You're right, Frank. There are so many here who do not know Jesus."

"To be sure we should stay here, but we will continue to pray. We won't say anything about Africa to anyone. If God wants us in Africa, let Him tell us and confirm it through someone else."

A short time passed. One Sunday morning following the service, God directed a retired minister, Rev. Haight (Hate), to speak to Frank.

"Good morning, Mr. Haight," greeted Frank.

"Good morning, pastor. Could I have a word with you?" inquired Mr. Haight.

"Sure," agreed Frank.

"I don't want you to think for a moment that we are not pleased to have you as our pastor. But the thought keeps coming to my mind that maybe God would have you be a missionary in Africa."

Frank stood speechless as Mr. Haight continued.

"I was wondering if He had been saying anything to you about that."

God had kept Africa in their thoughts and let them know that this was in His special plan through this dear friend.

There was so much to be done. Frank and Zola would have to finish their Bible school training at Fairmount. Papers would have to be filled out with the church headquarters. The United States government would have to grant a passport, permission for them to leave the country. And the Sierra Leone government would have to grant a visa, permission for them to enter and work in Sierra Leone.

Since it was at the close of World War I and the United States and Germany were still struggling over power, Frank and Zola had a difficult time convincing the government officials that their last name was Birch and not Bertch, a German spelling. They were questioned and had to take in evidence to show that Birch was their original name and it had not been changed.

Once the officers were satisfied, Frank and Zola had no further government delays.

Packing had to be done.

"Where do we begin?" asked Zola. "What should we take to Sierra Leone?"

"Let's visit the headquarters and talk with Rev. McCarty. I'm sure he will help us," suggested Frank.

Together they went to the headquarters to see Mr. McCarty.

"Well . . ." replied Rev. McCarty, "You will need just about everything – cots, chairs, dishes, food, clothing. The African people will not be able to offer you chairs, beds, or anything you have here so you'll have to take all necessary items."

"Will we be able to buy anything there?" asked Frank.

"There will be shops in the capital city of Freetown. You will be able to buy some meat, fresh fruits, cloth, kerosene for your lanterns, building supplies like cement, and tin sheeting for the roof," answered Mr. McCarty.

Excited and anxious to begin their packing, Frank and Zola returned home. Large wooden boxes were made to ship their supplies and furnishings. Several lists of needed items were written and checked over and over to be sure nothing was missing. They had packed everything they felt would be needed in Sierra Leone.

"Let's go over the list one more time, dear," suggested Frank.

Together they checked once more.

"Mattresses . . . cots . . . chairs . . . bedding . . . towels . . . wash cloths . . . toothpaste . . . dishes . . . silverware . . . pans . . . hurricane lanterns . . . food. . . ."

Chapter 4
We're Home

Frank and Zola sailed by ship to Freetown, Sierra Leone. Since there were no airlines and no direct ship routes, they sailed to England and then on to Sierra Leone. They were greeted warmly.

"Welcome! Welcome! I'm Birch Eddy and this is my wife, Dolly."

"I'm Frank Birch and this is my wife, Zola."

As soon as their supplies and luggage were unloaded, the national carriers assisted with the carrying of the load.

"Do they carry everything on their heads?" inquired Zola as she watched several lift the boxes to their heads.

"Oh, yes," replied Dolly. "They feel much more at ease carrying things that way."

As they walked along the red dirt road, Frank and Zola immediately began to notice differences in Sierra Leone compared to the States.

"Everything is so different here," stated Zola. "The people . . . the houses . . . the roads . . . the language. . . ."

"Don't worry about it, dear," encouraged Frank.

"We will help you get started in your work," added the Eddys.

"We want to learn all we can as fast as we can," said Frank. Turning to Zola he said, "We will be good Sierra Leoneans, Zola. You wait and see."

The Eddys were in charge of the mission work in Sierra Leone. To help Frank and Zola adjust as quickly as possible was their responsibility.

"We have a gift for you," announced the Eddys smiling.

"What kind of gift," inquired Frank and Zola.

"It is the best gift we know to give you."

"What could it be, Frank?" asked Zola as the Eddys went to say something to the carriers.

"Here is your gift," stated the Eddys as they returned with a national. "This is Mano (Mah-no). He is the best man around. He will turn word (interpret) for you, teach you the language, and help you get to know the people. He is a good man and will be a big help to you."

Frank and Zola thanked the Eddys for their kindness. At first the Birches could only guess about Mano's usefulness. But it wasn't long before they realized how valuable Mano would be.

Early one morning, the Birches and Eddys took the only train to Kamabai (Kah-mah-by). It was a very small and dusty train. There was an engine on each end. It stopped at several small villages. Each time the nationals would stare at them. The train windows were low and made it easy for the people to look in.

They bounced and swayed on the hard seats. They rode all day and night before reaching their stop. It seemed as though every muscle ached. They rested quite sometime and visited with the Limba people. Mano got them off to a good start in learning the language before they started for Kamakwie (Kah-mah-kwee).

Five missionaries were to make the trip to Kamakwie. They were: Miss Lulu Tanner, a nurse; Dr. Ruby Helen Paine, a doctor; Mr. Birch Eddy and the Birches.

"Are you ready?" called the men anxious to start the three-day trip to Kamakwie, the place where the Birches were to work.

"All set," replied Miss Tanner and Zola as they climbed in their hammocks.

"Are you sure these are safe?" asked Zola. "Won't the poles holding our hammocks slip off their heads?"

"You're safe, Zola," answered Miss Tanner. "Relax, the men know exactly what they are doing."

The Birches and others started the long journey with several nationals helping to carry the boxes and the women. They had just gotten on their way when Frank hurt his knee and had to be carried. Being a large man, he found this to be an embarrassment. The ladies willingly took turns being carried, walking, or riding Frank's horse.

The bush path began to narrow as they traveled. Overhanging elephant grass and weeds almost made the path disappear. The struggle to travel on a hot day caused them to stop often to rest.

"Miss Tanner, tell me about the people," said Zola. "What will we see when we get to Kamakwie?"

"Well, first you will notice that the people will stare at you. Many have never seen white people and you will seem strange to them. They will be somewhat shy until you have proven your love."

"How can I prove that I love them?" asked Zola.

"You are such a loving person, Zola. I'm sure that they will trust you as they get to know you better.

"What are their homes like?" quizzed Zola.

"The sundried mud walls are supported with an

inner frame made of sticks tied with vines. The roofs are grass. The floors are hard mud. Most of the homes have a front porch called a veranda."

"Do the homes have chairs or beds?" asked Zola.

"No, they wouldn't have those. Some will have a hammock, but that would be all," answered Miss Tanner.

As the party journeyed, Zola and Frank asked many questions about the people.

"Tell us about the families," encouraged the Birches. They listened as the Eddys shared about the people.

"In Sierra Leone so many little babies die that mothers can only hope they will live. The mother will have a clean headtie (one yard square of colored cloth) ready in which to wrap the baby. No name is given until the family is sure it won't die. In some areas you will find that a name is given when the father can buy a goat or sheep for a sacrifice."

"What if the baby lives? Do they have good homes?" asked Frank.

"The family usually pays a lot of attention to the little ones. When the children reach the age of two or three, they are corrected for everything – big or small. Often the mother will send her baby to her brother for training. She feels he would make her child mind better. The brother, in turn, will send his children to her. Most children are not raised in their own homes."

"What do the people do all day?" inquired Zola.

"The women and children do most of the work. The woman gets up early and sweeps the front porch and makes a fire. She fixes something for her family to eat, but she usually does not eat until later in the morning. The day is filled with pounding rice, looking after the fire or working in the rice fields."

"And the men?" questioned Frank.

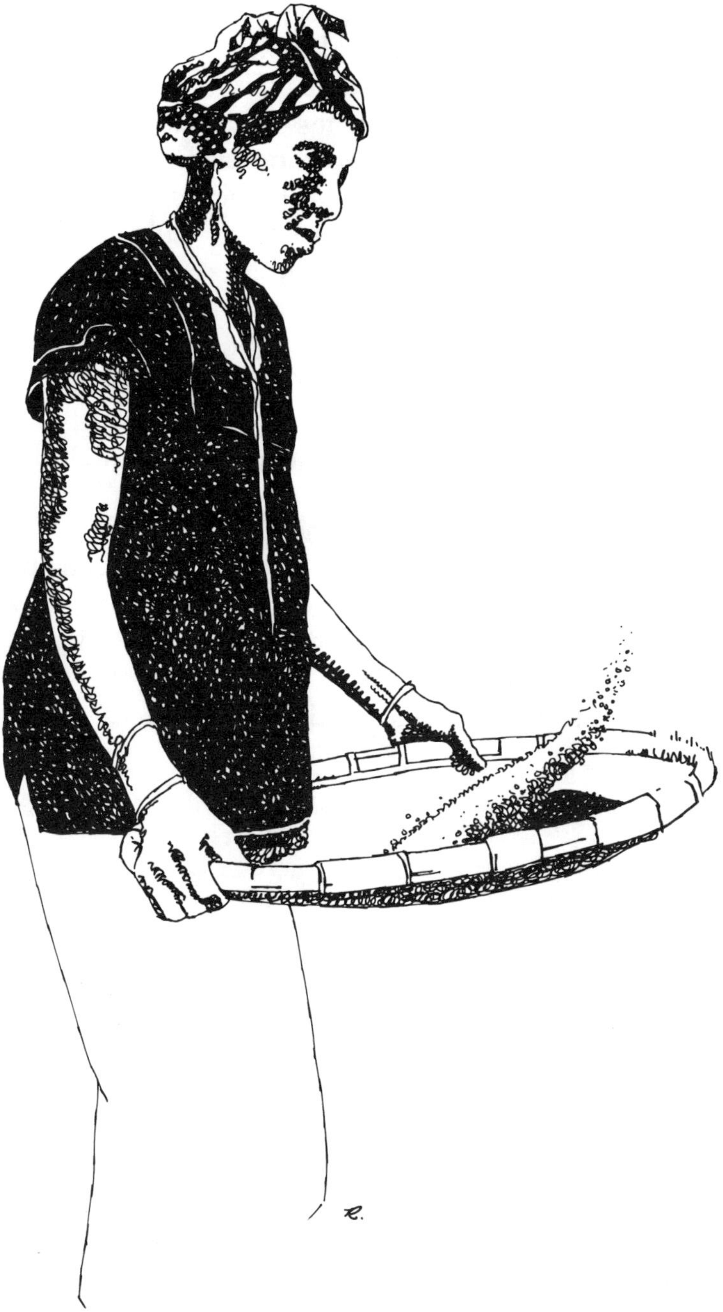

"The men make the decisions, hold town meetings, and watch the rice fields. The rice fields are outside of the villages. The men and boys build small houses on stilts close by to watch the fields. They make sling shots like David used. They shoo away the rice-eating birds and small animals such as monkeys."

"Frank, over there! What is that?" Zola whispered.

"I don't see anything, Zola."

"It was probably an animal," said Birch Eddy. "You will see many animals — monkeys, leopards, antelope, and elephants in certain areas."

"Oh, yes, you will also see rats, snakes, lizards, crickets, driver ants, and mosquitoes," added Dr. Paine cheerfully.

"You'll get used to it," encouraged Mr. Eddy.

The party walked three days before reaching the small clearing of Kamakwie. They were tired, hot and covered with scratches and marks from the sharp edges of the elephant grass blades.

Frank gave Zola's hand a little squeeze, "We're home, dear."

Chapter 5

Lots of Love

Kamakwie was a village of about 40 houses. Each house had 15 to 20 in the family. Mano and some of the carriers had gone ahead of the party to tell the people the white missionaries were coming. The drums could be heard from a distance. They were welcoming the missionaries. They stopped beating about 36 hours later!

Most children had a charm or two hanging around their necks. Many had large swollen stomachs from not eating the right food. The women wore long skirts called lapas and loose-flowing blouses called dockets. The men wore long robes.

Mr. Eddy introduced the Birches to the chief and his people. "They have come to bring you God's message and to help you," he said.

After friendly greetings and a short message from the Bible, it was time to show the Birches to their new home. They had known that the first few months would be hard and things would not be the same as in the States. Their first house was made of upright poles held in place with limber cross sticks tied with vines. The framework was supported with well-mixed mud balls which dried in position. The outside was then covered with a mixture of dirt, water and cow dung to keep the mud from breaking off or dusting. The inside walls were covered with a plasterlike mixture. The roof was cone-shaped and covered with grass. There were no screens for the windows or doors. Mosquito nets were used for protection at night.

"Pa Birch" said Mano. (Pa was said to give respect to a man. Ya was said to give respect to a woman.)

"Yes, Mano," answered Pa Birch.

"We must go and see the head man. He will tell us if you can stay here in Kamakwie."

Mano introduced Mr. Birch to Alimami Sedu (seh-doo), one of the leading men. Alimami Sedu had traveled some and been to Freetown where he had a good business and contact with white people. He did not trust all of them but did agree to let the Birches stay for a time.

Over the weeks that passed, a bond of love and respect grew between the Birches and the people. Although the Birches had not been trained as doctors, they did what they could to help the sick. They cleaned sores and wounds, gave out medicines for various sicknesses, wrapped injuries, helped the mothers with small children, and gave lots of love.

Pa Birch would have to meet the paramount (chief over everyone) chief for permission to stay in Kamakwie. Mano, Pa Birch, and Alimami Sedu went to the chief.

"Well, Alimami Sedu," said the chief, "What do you say about this man? You have been with him for a few weeks. Is he a good person for us?"

"Yes," replied Alimami Sedu. "I think he comes with the right heart. He does not come to do us bad."

"Do you really mean what you say?" questioned the chief.

"Yes, I do," answered Alimami Sedu. "He would be good for us."

"Well, if that is the case, you will leave your business in Freetown and stay in Kamakwie and help this man in his settling," commanded the chief.

That was a true test for Alimami Sedu. He had a good business in Freetown and this would mean a big loss of money. He did feel that Pa Birch would be good for Kamakwie. He left his business and spent the rest of his life in Kamakwie helping the Birches much of the time.

Mano was careful to see to it that the Birches boiled all of their water before drinking so they wouldn't get sick. A well was dug immediately so they wouldn't have to get their drinking water from the river.

Plans were made to build a new house. The building supplies had to be purchased in Freetown and carried from Kamabai. One day the carriers saw a big python snake about 18-20 feet long. It had swallowed a sheep and curled to sleep and digest its supper. The carriers killed the snake, left their loads, and went back to the village with the snake.

When the carriers didn't come, Pa Birch became worried. He sent a messenger to find them. The messenger found them in the village eating snake stew and rice. After losing a day and a night, the messenger insisted that they carry the loads to Kamakwie.

The Sierra Leone people could neither read nor write. They had not heard about Jesus and how He had died for their sins. The Birches read the Bible over and over to the people so they could remember what it said. The people were like small birds waiting to be fed. They were hungry to hear more about Jesus. Up until this time, there was no missionary stationed in their village. God knew the people's needs and which missionaries to send to love the people.

There was no hospital near to Kamakwie. When it came close to time for Mrs. Birch to have her baby, she traveled to Freetown. The Birches had wondered about the possibility of twins, but didn't think about it seriously. Marion was born first and Marilyn came three hours later. Mrs. Birch was very ill when the twins were born. Ice was needed, but none could be found. There were no ice boxes or refrigerators. The doctor sent messengers to others asking for ice, but there didn't seem to be any in Freetown. Again the messengers were sent. At last ice was found where some British soldiers were staying. One of the doctors sent a messenger and made plans for the ice to be sent to the hospital for Mrs. Birch. God had helped them find the ice, and Mrs. Birch began to get better slowly.

Chapter 6
No Repeat Performance

The little twins were normal – they saw everything, were into everything, and ate everything. Kelitege (Kel-eh-tee-gee) was hired to watch the twins while Mrs. Birch worked in the clinic helping sick people and Mr. Birch traveled to visit and preach in the villages. The twins loved to explore as Kelitege did the laundry by the water. He gathered water in large tubs, added soap to the clothes, and then rubbed them on large rocks. The twins watched him and others as they rubbed and rubbed. Some of the black boys and girls would play in the river and then get some water to take home for drinking, cooking, or bathing small children.

There was a pretty blue tablet that Kelitege used in the rinse water. It was poisonous. When he looked for the tablet, he didn't see it. He looked all around the rocks and water. It just disappeared. Then he saw the twins. Both had a pretty blue ring around their lips.

"Oh, no," thought Kelitege, "They ate it!"

He hurried the twins to Mrs. Birch.

"Ya Birch! Ya Birch! The twins ate the blue tablet that I use in the rinse water!" he panted to get the words out after running all the way. "Will they die, Ya? Will they die?" Kelitege was scared.

Mrs. Birch was scared. She would have to make them vomit to get as much of the chloride of mercury out of their bodies as possible. She quickly gave them something to make them sick. Then she gave them plenty of milk to help the tablet clot and not be absorbed by the body.

Mrs. Birch prayed and watched the twins all night. She didn't know that Kelitege was outside waiting, listening, and trying to figure out what was going on. As the sun began to rise, Kelitege knocked.

"Ya Birch, are the children here?" asked Kelitege.

"Yes, Kelitege, they are here. Come in."

"Are they all right?" he questioned.

"Yes. They are fine," answered Mrs. Birch.

"My heart is happy," replied Kelitege. "I will watch them much closer, Ya Birch. They will not eat the tablet again," assured Kelitege.

The twins, not knowing what the tablet was, decided it didn't taste good enough to go through eating it again.

There was another time that the twins decided that they would not repeat what they had done. Mother had warned them several times not to touch the lovely red hot peppers which grew on a bush near the house.

She repeated over and over, "Do not pick the peppers. Do not put them in your mouth."

But the peppers were so pretty and well within reach. The twins didn't realize that the peppers were the hottest on earth. They couldn't understand how something so pretty could not be good to eat.

Marion picked one and shared it with Marilyn. They cried and cried and cried. When little ones cry, they rub their eyes, and that's what the twins did. The more

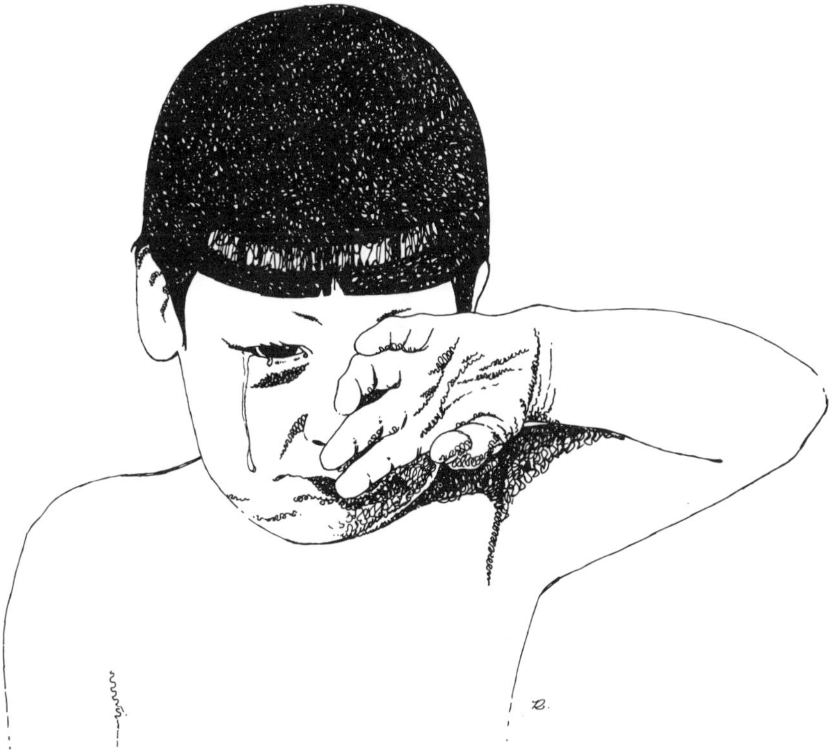

they rubbed, the more the pepper burned their eyes. They had burning eyes and mouths.

Mrs. Birch cooked clean rags in milk and made the twins suck on them. This helped a little. Kelitege saw the twins sucking on the rags and knew that they shouldn't be putting things in their mouths. Not knowing why the twins had the rags, he took them away. The crying started all over again. Mrs. Birch came to their rescue and explained to Kelitege what had happened.

The twins suffered no damage to their eyes or lining of their mouths. They never bothered the peppers again.

Sierra Leone has army ants also called "driver ants." Thousands of these ants travel on a narrow path about an inch wide. Each side of the path is guarded by the male soldier ants. These guards stand upright, with arms steadying one another and their large tweezer mouths are spread open ready to bite anything that bothers them. The mother and baby ants travel between the guard lines on both sides of their little highway. They do not like anyone or anything to bother them. They eat small animals, like rats, and any dead animals in their path.

Like all little children, the twins wandered away from the house one day. They came across a path of these ants and decided to investigate. They could have stepped over but went through them instead. The ants crawled all over them and started to bite. The twins cried and cried.

A neighbor lady saw the twins and their problem. She grabbed them, removed all of their clothing and picked off all the ants she could find. Since the Birches were the only white family in the area, she had no problem knowing to whom the twins belonged. The twins were upset and crying, but they were safe from the ants.

Chapter 7
Two of Everything

The twins were almost three when they returned to the States with their mother. Mrs. Birch was expecting a baby. The Birches talked about whether she should return to the States or go to Freetown hospital where the twins were born. Because she was so sick after the twins came, they decided Mrs. Birch and the twins would come back to the States.

The trip was made by ship. To the twins' delight, Mrs. Birch gave them a small gift each day. There were always two gifts – one for Marilyn and one for Marion. These small gifts helped the long hours pass a little quicker.

One day Mrs. Birch gave each a balloon. Marion got a red one, and Marilyn got a yellow one.

"Blow mine up, please," asked Marilyn.

"Mine, too," asked Marion.

Both children danced up and down as Mrs. Birch blew the balloons up and tied a string on them.

"Let me tie this around your wrist, Marilyn," suggested Mother.

Willingly, Marilyn held out her arm so the string could be tied.

"Here, Marion, let me tie your balloon on," said Mother.

"No, thank you. I can hold it," insisted Marion.

"It would be better if we tied it on," urged Mother.

"I don't want it tied," answered Marion.

Mrs. Birch didn't say anymore about the balloon. She watched the twins play with the balloons for several minutes. Suddenly a quick breeze picked up Marion's balloon, and it was out of his reach. He cried as though his heart would break. What made Marion unhappy also made Marilyn unhappy so she cried, too. As they watched the balloon bounce over the ocean, Mother joined them and tried to make them feel better.

"Wouldn't it be funny if a fish thought the balloon was something to eat and jumped up and grabbed it? The balloon would pop in its mouth!" said Mother.

The crying stopped and the twins watched and watched for a fish to jump at the balloon. Mrs. Birch had several ways of making things better.

Captain Holmes loved to play with the twins. He would chase them around the ship. He would run after them, letting the twins get ahead. He would then stop and run the opposite way. The ship was oblong and the twins didn't understand how he could get ahead of them.

He would gather them in his arms and say, "Oh Sunny Jim and Sister Sue, I'm going to gobble you up. I'll gobble you up. I will gobble you up."

Then he would squeeze and hug them. The twins giggled with glee.

Mrs. Birch and the twins lived with their grandparents while in the States. One morning Mrs. Birch called the twins to her.

"I'll be gone for a short while. When I get back, I'll have something for you," said Mother.

The twins knew that they would get something because Mother and Daddy had always given them something. Even short overnight trips brought them a sucker, balloon, or toy.

Early one morning Marilyn came down the stairs. Mother was by the pot-belly stove, their only source of heat, getting ready to give the new baby a bath. The baby was all red, kicking, and crying.

"Well, this is what I brought you, Marilyn," said Mother. "I told you I would bring you something."

"Where is the other one?" asked Marilyn. "You always bring two of everything."

"Oh, this is the only one I could find this time. You will have to share Larry with your brother," answered Mother.

The children were reminded daily about their Daddy. They had his picture and often talked about their Daddy in Africa. Almost two years passed without seeing him, and he became a bit hazy in their minds.

Mrs. Birch never complained about raising the children alone while Mr. Birch was working in Africa. She always looked on the bright side when they would be together as a family again. She felt sure that this was part of God's design for their lives, and this brought peace to her heart.

One bright morning, Marilyn got up and went downstairs. Both of her parents were by the stove. Her father was pulling on his socks. Marilyn did not know him without his glasses so she just stood there.

"Come kiss your daddy, Marilyn," urged Mother.

"Well, we have another daddy in Africa, haven't we?" asked Marilyn.

Her parents seemed to know that Marilyn didn't know him without his horn-rimmed glasses. As soon as he put his glasses on, Marilyn knew this man was her daddy.

"Marion isn't awake yet," said Mother. "Let's go upstairs and surprise him."

All three went to Marion's room.

"Wake up, Marion," said his mother gently shaking him.

Marion sat up in bed not quite awake.

"Here's your daddy, Marion."

The little fellow looked at his daddy and said, "Ah, come on. That's not Daddy."

Their father hadn't been forgotten. The twins just couldn't connect the picture with the real person. It took no time for them to feel like a family again.

Chapter 8
Confident in Their Trust

For the next few years, Mr. Birch traveled to different churches telling the people about Africa. During those times, Mrs. Birch worked hard at what she referred to as "raising twins and triplets." She taught the children many things. Scripture memory work was always part of their family devotions. By the time the twins started to school, they could say from memory Luke 2, the Christmas story. The teachers were so impressed that they had the twins visit each of the classrooms and recite the story.

After several years back in the States, the headquarters leaders wanted the Birches to serve in the mission work at Kamabai and later open a mission work in Binkola (Ben-kola). The Birches had many questions in their minds. At that time Sierra Leone was known as the white man's grave. It had a lot of swamps which were great places for mosquitoes to breed. The mosquitoes carried sickness and fevers which often led to death. It was not unusual for the men to leave their families safe in the States while they worked there. Many of our early Wesleyan missionaries died while in Sierra Leone.

"Frank, God has given us three beautiful children," said Mrs. Birch. "Should we take them back to Sierra Leone? Do you think this is in His best plan?"

Together they prayed about the decision. They knew that if God wanted them in Sierra Leone, He would make it clear; and they could trust that He would take care of them. All they needed to know was that God was leading them to make this move.

One morning during devotions, God spoke to Mrs. Birch through her Bible reading. She was reading about the Children of Israel wandering in the wilderness. God told them to send 12 spies into the Promised Land. Two of the spies were excited about what they saw and knew that God was able to help them take the land. The other ten spies could see only the strong, big men and the tall walls around the city.

The people agreed with the ten spies and refused to go. They began to complain and say they would have been better off to die in Egypt. They even used their wives and children as an excuse for not taking the land.

Tears filled Mrs. Birch's eyes as she read.

"Dear Lord, if Frank and I are about to behave in the same way of distrust in making our children an excuse in not following Your plan for our lives, we want to change our way right now. We believe that You can keep and bring us through any problems."

With her prayer came a feeling of peace. Mrs. Birch knew that God wanted them to return to Sierra Leone. After the Birches talked and prayed several more times together, they began to make plans to return. They knew that the trip might bring hardships, maybe sickness, and perhaps even death. They gave their children back to God and asked Him to watch and care for them.

There were no schools for Marion, Marilyn, and

Larry to attend in Sierra Leone so arrangements were made for them to take their studies through the mail. A package of books, paper and tests for each child was mailed to the Birches. The children were given a separate room in the house for studying and each had a desk. Mrs. Birch used a large blackboard as your teachers do.

Often there were times the lesson had to stop so Mrs. Birch could care for a person needing help. She didn't let the children skip the lesson though. She would help them study in the evenings until they caught up. School was school, and she kept them on schedule with their lessons.

All of the tests were mailed to Maryland for grading. The children always watched the mail for their grades. Both parents were quick to give them praise for doing well. Their parents wanted the children to have all the education possible so they would have trained minds with which to serve the Lord. Although the Birches never suggested what they would like for each child to be when they grew up, Mr. and Mrs. Birch spoke to the children often about God having a special design for their lives. The children grew up knowing that God loved them and was interested in what they became.

A boarding school for boys was started at Binkola. Each week the boys ate 600 pounds of rice, 60 pounds of meat, 30 pounds of peanuts, 18 pounds of salt, 30 pounds of okra or other greens, 48 pounds of dry lima beans, 7½ gallons of palm oil and 2 quarts of dry peppers. All of these items are used in the soup for the rice. It also took eight bars of soap, 2" x 2" x 12", for every boy to have a small piece for his weekly wash.

The Birch children enjoyed going with their parents to purchase needed supplies at the market. When entering the market, you would see dried fish, peppers, peanuts, eggs, spinach, potato leaves, tobacco rice, palm oil, cassava, native soap, oranges, bananas, avocado pears, limes, and eggplant. In one corner is some meat, probably a cow or maybe a goat or sheep.

"Misses, look my fine ground nut (peanut)," called one woman.

"Misses, good morning, look my fine eggs. You not go buy my fine fish?" called another.

Mrs. Birch stopped and purchased some eggs and then moved on through the market.

"Misses, look my fine spinach," called a man.

Shopping takes a long time. Because of the food needs, the Birches went to the market about twice a week.

Chapter 9

Separating the Sheep and Goats

Marilyn asked Jesus into her heart when she was eight. When her father was planning to baptize people at Kunso, our first Wesleyan mission in Sierra Leone, Marilyn asked to join them.

"Daddy, can I be baptized, too?" asked Marilyn.

"Do you know what it means to be baptized?" questioned her father.

"I think so," she replied.

"Tell me what it means, Marilyn."

"It means I have asked Jesus into my heart, that He forgave my sins, and I will obey and live for Him," answered Marilyn.

"That is right," he said. "When we are dipped under the water it represents that our sins have been forgiven. When we are brought up out of the water, it is telling others that we will live for Him."

So on a Sunday afternoon, Marilyn and 12 other African Christians were baptized in the Kunso stream.

One warm day when the twins were about ten, Marion and Marilyn were sitting on the front porch of the little mission house. Mrs. Birch was busy on the inside and Mr. Birch was visiting villages and preaching.

Marion and Marilyn were watching the sheep, goats, chickens and skinny dogs roam about the yard.

"Marion, you know what?" said Marilyn.

"What?" asked Marion.

"These sheep and goats remind me of the Lord's parable," answered Marilyn.

"Which parable?" asked Marion.

"You remember. The one which talks about the judgment day. The goats and sheep are together, but God separates them. God says, 'Welcome to my kingdom,' to the sheep and 'I really don't know you and you will have no part in my kingdom,' to the goats.

Suddenly Marion jumped up crying and went into the house. Marilyn, not sure what was said to upset him, followed.

"Mother, I want to be saved," cried Marion. "I don't want to be like the goats and not be able to enter heaven."

Together they prayed and Marion's sins were forgiven.

The three children were good to help their parents with the mission work. Each Sunday they would get up very early and travel with their mother and friends down what looked like a road. There were five large villages down that road. They would pass by the first village. Each child, with a national friend, was left at a different village. Then Mrs. Birch went to the fifth village. Each held a simple service in Limba. They sang songs, told Bible stories and taught Scripture verses.

Mrs. Birch would come back and pick up each child. All of them would then stop at the first village for another service. They would arrive back in Binkola just in time for the morning service.

Little girls in Africa usually helped with the chores, cooking or laundry. This left Marilyn to play alone most of the time. She busied herself with reading and writing to pen pals. Her letters helped to keep the family in touch with what was happening in the States.

Marilyn also loved to take pictures. Mrs. Birch would often give her tips. She learned how to decide what she wanted in the picture and to leave the other things out. For a feeling of depth in a picture, she learned to have something in the picture near while focusing on something else farther away.

Marion and Larry played with the African boys much of their free time. They learned to speak Limba and Temne (Tem-ne) quickly. They had no problems in knowing what the people were saying.

Whatever Marion did, Larry wanted to do the same. Both of the boys loved to play soccer. They became very good at using their feet, heads and bodies to move the ball. The boys also loved to go hunting with their father. They learned to handle the guns well.

One day Marion went hunting with a couple of African boys. The family thought he would get a bush fowl or ground squirrel. When he returned, he brought back an antelope. Everyone was delighted. This would make many good meals.

Chapter 10
Elephant Hunting

"Konk! Konk! Pa Birch!" called the messenger. (Most Africans do not have wooden doors to knock on so they call "Konk! Konk!")

"I'm Pa Birch," said Mr. Birch going to the door.

"This letter is for you," said the messenger.

Mr. Birch took the letter and began to read.

Dear Mr. Birch,
    We send you and your family special greetings.
    The people from a little village in Tonko country have sent word to us that a mean elephant is bothering them. It has destroyed their gardens, trampled the huts and even killed someone. Everytime it sees a person, it charges.
    We are hoping that you can help us. Please take this big elephant gun I am sending with this messenger and kill the elephant. We have heard how well you can shoot.
    Be careful for the elephant is very dangerous. Thank you for doing this.

                              District Commissioner

Mrs. Birch had listened while he read the letter.

"Oh, Frank, I don't think you should go after a bad elephant like that. What if it charges you? Or suppose it tramples you?" Mrs. Birch shook with the terrible thoughts.

"Dear, I'll be fine. If the elephant is going to kill others, I should go and try to kill it. Please pray with me before I go."

They prayed together asking God to help him find and kill the bad elephant. They asked God to protect Mr. Birch and the other hunters.

As he did when visiting villages, Mr. Birch went about the house collecting enough supplies for several days and packing them in a chop box (usually made of thin boards).

"Let's see . . . I'll need this . . . and some canned food . . . a couple of lanterns . . . kerosene . . . knives . . . tent and cots," he thought to himself.

"Can we go along, Dad?" asked Marion and Larry.

"Not this time, boys," answered their father. "The elephant is mean and dangerous."

"Please, Dad," insisted the boys.

"No, sons. You cannot go this time. Stay here and take care of things while I'm gone."

With two nationals to help track and carry supplies, Mr. Birch set out to find the elephant. They walked several days in the hot, melting sun before reaching Tonko country. They tried to rest at night, but they felt uneasy with the mean elephant somewhere close by.

"I wonder why the elephant turned mean?" thought Mr. Birch out loud.

"Some who have seen it say it has a broken tusk. It may have a giant toothache that is driving it mad," suggested Bai (By).

"Some people say it has an evil spirit," answered Sorie (Soo-ree).

"Pa Birch," asked Bai. "How are we going to find and kill this elephant without him charging us?"

"I'm not sure how to answer you. We will have to wait until we find it," replied Mr. Birch.

The men struggled through miles of elephant grass, grass which grows as high as telephone poles. They had followed the elephant's tracks but hadn't seen any elephant. Mr. Birch had a feeling that they were getting close. Bai, the tracker, took the lead. Following the fresh tracks, Bai signaled for everyone to move as quietly as possible so the elephant would not hear them.

One of the men spotted a nearby tree and motioned that he would climb it for a better view. Slowly he walked to the tree and climbed above the grass. He signaled that the mean elephant and two more were just ahead.

Quietly, the men decided what they would do.

"If we go around the elephants to the hill behind, perhaps we can get a better view," suggested one.

Trying to make no noise and staying far enough away so the elephants couldn't smell them, the men worked their way to the hill.

"Oh, this is a good spot," whispered Mr. Birch.

The big, mean elephant was standing in a small clearing just ahead. Its big ears flapped back and forth, back and forth.

"Can you shoot it?" asked Sorie.

"I should be able to get it. You two be ready to run," urged Mr. Birch. "The other two elephants may charge."

Mr. Birch prayed a short prayer as he took careful aim. His finger gently pressed the trigger. Boom! The huge rifle almost leaped out of his hands. The kick of the gun rocked Frank back. The second elephant stood

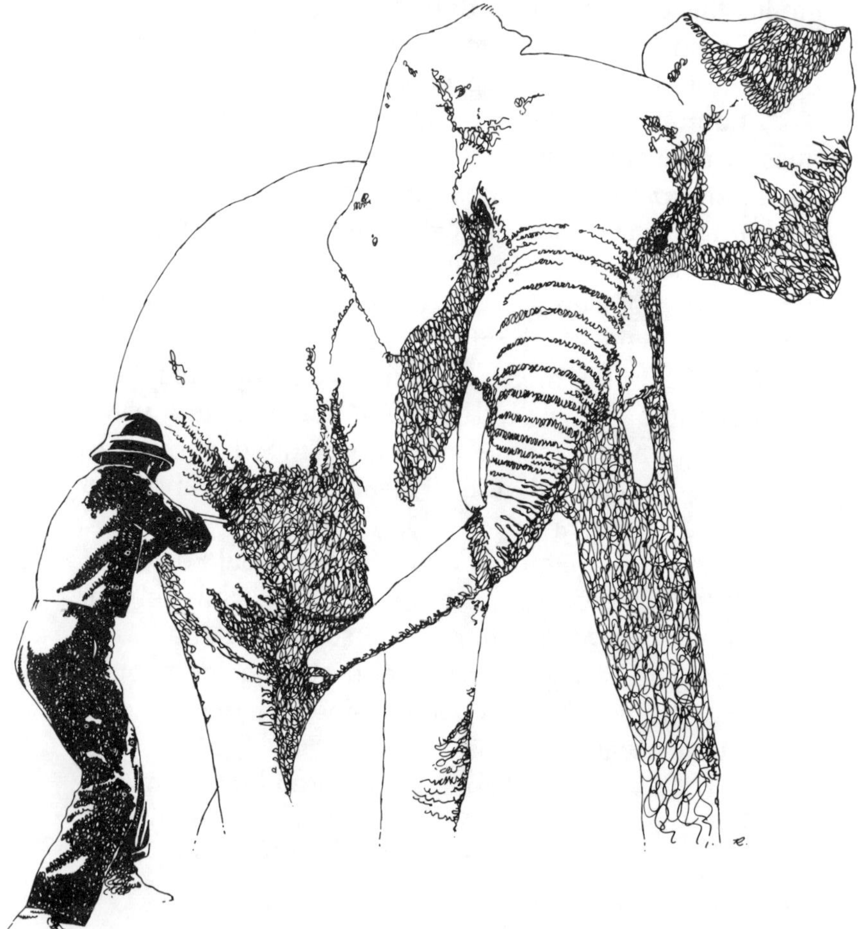

and charged, and Mr. Birch shot it. The third elephant had already headed for him. God helped Mr. Birch not to panic. He took careful aim and shot. All three elephants were dead.

"Thank you, God," he said as he sat down. He felt a bit shaky after all the excitement was over.

People began coming from all the surrounding villages. They chopped up the meat with large knives and carried it home to eat. Everyone was happy that the mean elephant was dead, and that they would have plenty of meat for awhile.

Chapter 11

A Broken Heart

The Birch family returned to the States in time for the twins to enter their second year of high school. Their first year had been completed in Sierra Leone through the mail. Both of the Birches felt a deep responsibility to train their children and had given them the best schooling possible.

During that second year of high school, Mr. Birch received an invitation to take a pastorate in a college town. Mr. and Mrs. Birch were excited about the possibility. This would mean that the children could live at home, and the parents would be able to help them through high school and college. The family began to pray about the move.

Also during that same year, the Birches were contacted about returning to Sierra Leone. Now they would have to make a choice. Should they return to Sierra Leone or take the pastorate?

"I don't know what we should do, Frank," stated Mrs. Birch. "I would love for you to take that pastorate so the children could live with us through their college years."

"I know, Zola," replied Mr. Birch, "but I'm not

sure about taking it."

"If we return to Sierra Leone, we would have to leave our children here. I don't want to do that," said Mrs. Birch.

"I don't want to leave them either," agreed Mr. Birch. "Let's pray about it and see what God wants. He will make His plan clear to us."

The Birches prayed and talked and prayed and talked. Both decided they must stay in the States and help their children through high school and college. The decision was made, and they would have to talk with Dr. McCarty at the church headquarters about not returning to Sierra Leone.

Mr. and Mrs. Birch started the trip to headquarters by car. Not far from home, they hit a slick patch of ice on the road and the car rolled over. Neither of the Birches was hurt so they got out. Some people who had stopped to help gave them a hand in turning the car back over. The car had a number of dents and scraches but ran fine so they headed back home.

A couple of weeks later they started to make the trip again. They had only driven a few miles when a blizzard hit. They were forced to turn back and find a motel for the night. The next day they returned home.

By this time, Mr. and Mrs. Birch were beginning to feel as though they should double check their decision with God. They thought they were taking the right action by staying in the States, but perhaps God had another plan.

"Dear Father," prayed Mrs. Birch. "If we are about to make the wrong decision, please show us. If You want us to return to Sierra Leone, would You please let someone be saved in the Sunday evening service."

Mrs. Birch did not share her prayer with anyone. She knew that her husband usually had a Bible study or a message for those who already knew Jesus as their

Savior on Sunday evenings. The church had more visitors on Sunday mornings, and it would be more likely for him to have an altar call then.

That Sunday evening, Mr. Birch preached a message to the Christians, but felt that he should give an altar call. When he asked for those who wanted Jesus to come into their hearts to come forward, one young man went to the altar.

"Oh, Father," gasped Mrs. Birch as she realized what this could mean. "Dear Father," she prayed. "If You are trying to tell us to return to Africa, would You confirm it by sending yet another one tonight to seek You?"

Down the aisle walked another man.

"Oh, Father . . ." thought Mrs. Birch as she could not overlook the second young man.

The Birches continued to pray. They felt that they should return to Sierra Leone, but still there was the question about the children.

Where would they live and who would care for them?

Mr. and Mrs. Birch had learned about a boarding school in South Carolina. It was for missionary children whose parents were overseas. After visiting the school, arrangements were made for the children to go there. Mrs. Birch remained with the children until the school year started while Mr. Birch sailed on to Sierra Leone.

There was a guest house on the school grounds. Mrs. Birch stayed there at night while the children stayed in their dorm rooms. It was very hard for her to think about leaving the children. She had hidden her crying heart from them. The pain of separating for two years increased as the last day drew closer.

The last night before she left, Mrs. Birch returned to the guest house and cried. She knelt down beside the bed and sobbed. She felt as though her heart would break as she opened it before God.

"Dear Father, if there is any healing for a broken heart, I must have it tonight or I'll never be able to leave those three children in the morning."

God touched her broken heart and gave her a special peace. She was able to sleep well through the night. He had heard her cry and answered.

The children and Mrs. Birch said their farewells the next morning. No one would have ever known of the "hurt" that was hers the night before. She would miss her children dearly, but she had placed them in God's hands. God would take care of them as she followed Him with her husband in Sierra Leone.

Chapter 12
No Passage Out

Marion met Marjorie at the boarding school. All of the children stayed in a big, two-story dorm. The girls were on one side and the boys on the other. On the third evening after the Birch children arrived, there was an open house and small groups visited the other side of the dorm. Marion saw Marjorie and knew that he would like to get to know her better. Since the young ladies and young men were not to write notes, walk together or hold hands, Marion and Marjorie would talk at meals or greet each other as they passed on the grounds.

The boarding school kept about 90 children. The youngest children were in kindergarten and the older ones were in high school or Bible school. There were usually two children in each room. Each was to follow the same time schedule. They got up at 5:30 and had one-half an hour to get ready for school, brush their teeth and clean their rooms. An inspection was made of each room. At 6:00 the older children had a book of Bible questions to work. The Bible references were given with the questions so they could look the answers up and write them in the book. Breakfast was served at 7:00 in a large basement room in another building. Everyone ate their meals together.

Most of the children went to school on the grounds. There was a short rest time in the afternoon and at least two hours of work. The children washed and dried dishes, set the tables, fixed shoes, worked in the yard, picked pecans, cleaned rooms, mended clothes, and whatever needed to be done. One of Marion's jobs was to watch a small group of younger children and keep them out of trouble. Larry became quite an expert in binding old school books.

At Christmastime, all the goodies were kept together in one store room. Each of the children were encouraged to share the things they received since not everyone received the same. If one felt selfish and wanted to keep something just for himself, he had to write, "FOR ME ONLY" or "FOR ME, MYSELF, & I" on the box. This was a rule to help the children to learn to share with others who didn't have as much.

Right after the Sunday noon meal, the children had a prayer and letter-writing time. Since their parents were stationed all over the world doing missionary work, the children shared their parents' joys and prayer requests. It was encouraging for the Birch children to hear how God was working in different countries. After prayer, they would write to their parents.

Mrs. Birch was the main letter writer. She wrote every week. Because the mail was sent by ship, often her letters would come two or three at a time. The Birch children would get together and read them over and over.

The Birches had hoped to be back in the States in time to start the twins in college. That was not possible because no one could enter or leave the country when World War II broke out. The coast of Freetown was full of British ships. The British were using it as a military post. The mail was checked so the Birches could not tell the children what was happening.

One day the mail brought the Birches two envelopes. One was from Dr. McCarty at the headquarters and the other one was from the children. The letter from Dr. McCarty said that he could not find anyone to take their place in Sierra Leone and no passage out of the country could be obtained. He wanted to know if they would please stay longer.

Each child, not knowing what the others had written, wrote about the same things. Mrs. Birch's eyes filled with tears as she read each letter.

Dear Mother and Dad:
I miss you so much. I wish you could be here with us. I know you are needed there. Your work is so important. If you find that you need to stay longer, I will understand. God will help us and we will be fine.

Mrs. Birch took the four letters and spread them out on the table where she often talked with God.

"Dear Father, I know that You know what is in these letters. Would You please read them once again and help Frank and me to know Your plan and what You want done."

God answered, "Well, Mrs. Birch, I know you are concerned about your children. If you could have anything, what would you ask for them?"

"Father, I would like to ask for Houghton College for all three of them, the University of Michigan Medical School for Marilyn and whatever the boys will need when the time comes."

A peace filled her heart, and she knew that God would work everything out for the children's educations, and God would answer her prayer.

The children moved to Houghton, New York, when the twins finished high school. God provided a place for them to live as they went to college. The twins were first assigned rooms in the girls' dorm. When the twins sent their papers in, someone thought Marion was a girl and assigned him a room with a girl named Beulah. It caused quite a stir when they discovered Marion was a young man.

A close friend of their mother's opened up her home near the college and invited the three Birch children to live with her. This they did until their parents returned during the last semester of college for the twins.

Chapter 13
God's Design for Frank and Zola

Frank Birch started following God when only a young man. Only God knew the special design that could be made from his yielded heart and life. What a beautiful design God made.

The years that Frank and Zola Birch spent in Sierra Leone were not easy ones since much of the mission work was new. Frank Birch spent many, many days out visiting the villages and becoming acquainted with the people. He knew that he would have to earn their trust before they would listen about Jesus. Whenever someone needed a helping hand, he was always there.

The planning of new churches and mission stations, telling the people about Jesus, and teaching school were left to Frank and Zola. They were very loving and giving people and tried to minister to the hurting people.

There were many disappointments and many good times. Frank and Zola had learned very early in life that they could lean on Jesus when things weren't going so well. They knew that they were doing His will by serving in Sierra Leone.

Mr. Birch was elected general secretary of the world missions department at headquarters during their last term of serving in Sierra Leone. He served in that position until he retired 16 years later. He loved the work of missions and felt a deep concern for the missionaries. One of his dreams was for a special retirement center where the missionaries could live. Many of the missionaries had given all of their lives serving overseas and had come back to the States with no family to care for them. This was a big concern to Mr. Birch.

The Brooksville community was started for retired missionaries. Today our missionaries and many others enjoy the Florida climate.

Mr. Birch was also very interested in the merger between the Wesleyan Methodist and Pilgrim Holiness Churches. He did not live to attend the conference but actively took part in exploring the possibilities and making preparations for it.

Chapter 14

God's Design for Marion

Juniors and seniors at the boarding school were sent out in teams to nearby homes. Marion and several others walked a couple of miles to do a Sunday school lesson each week for a family with four children. This gave him practice in talking with people about God and sharing the Bible.

As prayer requests were given by the other children at the boarding school, Marion felt the need to be alone to pray. Often he would go to his room and pray for several minutes. It was during these special prayer times that God began to speak to him about his future and doing missionary work.

Marion loved to sing. He had two music teachers that helped him with his music. One wanted him to enter a solo contest at Clemson University in South Carolina as well as sing in the school choir. This would mean that he would have to get permission from the boarding school to go a day early. The lady in charge would not let him go early but did agree to let him sing with the school choir. Marion was disappointed he could not enter the solo contest. The choir won first place which pleased him.

When the twins entered Houghton College, Larry enrolled in the Houghton Academy. Marion had to separate from Marjorie since she went to California for more education. They wrote letters while apart.

Marion joined the Wesleyan church at Houghton and was given the job as director of YMWB and led missions in Sunday school. Once a month before Sunday school started, Marion had something special about missions. He purchased a set of books on famous missionaries for the YMWBers to read. Young YMWBers enjoy and like to pattern their lives after heroes. Marion hoped that some of his YMWBers would follow into missionary work.

During Marion's second year of college, Marjorie moved to Philadelphia and he bought a small barber shop. He charged 35¢ for each hair cut. If he worked 24 to 28 hours each week, it gave him enough money to go see Marjorie once every two or three months.

While on vacation from college between his junior and senior years, Marion stayed with a friend and worked in a greenhouse. It was hard work. To have time alone with God, Marion would walk. He loved to talk with God especially when things troubled him.

"Father," said Marion as he kicked at the rocks, "Marjorie is coming tomorrow for a visit. . . . We have been writing for a very long time. . . . Am I serious about her? . . . Should I ask her to marry me? . . . What about my education? . . . Maybe I should finish college and then go on to get another degree. . . . Are you asking me to be a missionary in Sierra Leone? . . ."

Marion was full of questions and very confused. God didn't give any direct answers, but He gave Marion a peace in his heart. Marion was so happy that God had touched him that he danced around, laughed, sang, and cried. God would take care of him and answer his questions as needed. Marion knew that God would be with him as he took each new step.

Marion was staying by a lake. One beautiful evening, he took Marjorie out in a canoe. The sunset painted the sky with streaks of yellow, orange, gray, and white. The blue water gently splashed against the boat as Marion and Marjorie enjoyed God's handiwork.

It seemed to be just the right time so Marion asked Marjorie if she would marry him. She was excited and said that she would.

Marion graduated from Houghton College the middle of May and was married a couple of days later. The door opened for Marion to go on to Wheaton, Illinois, for more education before going to Sierra Leone.

Marion and Marjorie served in Sierra Leone in many ways. They taught in the Bible school helping to train pastors for the many people who wanted to hear about God. It was hard for the people to understand the meaning of the English words so Marion began to translate God's Word into Temne, the trade language.

Marjorie made charts and worked with the ladies. She told them Bible stories using flannelgraph pictures to help them understand what she was saying.

Filmstrips and slides were helpful in their public services. Marion and Marjorie always tried to tell the people about Jesus and their need to be saved, that their sins could be forgiven because of Jesus dying for them and they could live pleasing to Him because He watches over them.

Marion and Marjorie knew that the people needed to hear God's Word in their own language. He helped to build a radio station so more would be able to hear. He also sent out teams of Bible school students to go into parts of the country where there was no mission work or the people didn't have a pastor. During the dry season, teams of students went out to villages. They stayed in two villages ten days each, took a ten-day rest, and then went on to two more villages.

Today Marion and Marjorie live in Texas. They still enjoy traveling around the United States telling people about Sierra Leone and the work of missions.

Chapter 15

God's Design for Marilyn

Marilyn's first memories of someone talking about missionaries goes back to when her mother was a YMWB director. Her mother made the stories come alive for the children. Memorizing Scripture verses and praying for the missionaries were always a part of the YMWB service. Marilyn always looked forward to the services.

Whether in the States or Sierra Leone, the Birch family loved to open their home to guests. They always made visitors feel welcome and enjoyed their company. Dr. Mabel Silver was a physician serving in Sierra Leone. She became a family friend and visited when possible. She was a cheerful, jolly lady who loved to tell the children stories.

Marilyn's thoughts turned toward medical work at an early age. The visits of Dr. Silver helped her decide for sure. Dr. Silver loved her medical work and never let on that it was a hardship or she was tired of the people coming by the hundreds day after day. She had trained to be a medical missionary and knew that God wanted her to serve Him through her medicine and love.

Marilyn knew that this was what she wanted to do. She went to Houghton College and the University of Michigan Medical School for several years of training before returning to Sierra Leone as a doctor.

There were hundreds of people who came daily for treatment. Each one was to register and get a card with a number on it. They then tried to find a place to sit down in the open waiting area. The backless benches were crowded with men, women, and children. A few chickens were scattered about the room.

Each patient was taken to a small side room and checked by a nurse. If the case was serious, Dr. Birch was called. Rebekah was one of Dr. Birch's patients.

"And who do we have here?" inquired Dr. Birch as she entered the small examination room.

Nine-year-old Rebekah opened her mouth but no sound came out.

"She cannot talk," answered her father. "We were eating and she got something caught in her throat."

Dr. Birch took Rebekah's chin in her hand. Smiling and giving Rebekah a little wink she asked, "Let me see if I can find the problem."

Carefully searching for something uncommon, Dr. Birch continued talking with Rebekah's father. "How long has she been this way?"

"A month," he replied. "Our neighbors say she has a witch sickness and the white man's medicine cannot help. They say only our people with special powers can help her."

"Do you believe what they say," asked Dr. Birch.

"Oh, no," he replied quickly. "I am a Christian. I know that God will help her."

"I will have to make Rebekah sleep so I can check her throat," insisted Dr. Birch.

"Will she feel pain?"

"No, she will not feel anything," answered Dr.

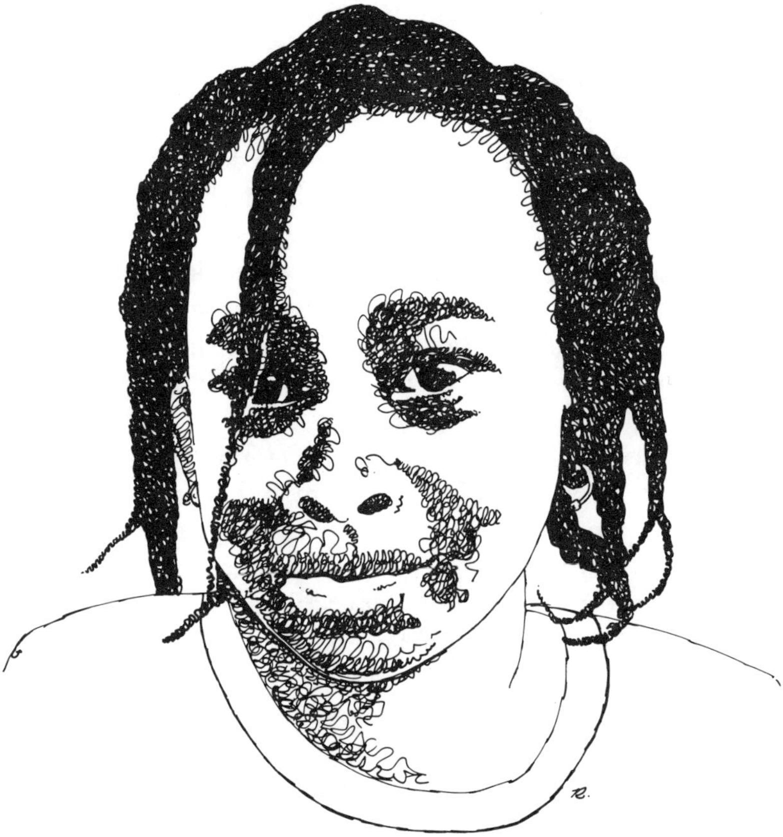

Birch. "From her chart I see you have come a great distance."

"We live in a village about 40 miles away."

"Can I stay while you check her throat?" asked her father.

"No, you will need to wait outside. Let's pray before we begin."

Dr. Birch prayed with the anxious father and frightened Rebekah. She assured both of them that Rebekah would be fine.

The nurse put a needle into Rebekah's arm. In only a couple of minutes she was asleep. Her head was tilted back. Dr. Birch inserted an instrument down the throat searching for what was blocking the vocal cords.

"I don't see anything," said Dr. Birch as she continued to probe carefully. "There must be something caught in there."

Dr. Birch searched for several minutes but could not find anything blocking the vocal cords.

"I'm sorry," she told Rebekah's father. "I could not find the problem. Perhaps if we wait, whatever it is will pass."

"What if it doesn't?" he inquired.

"Bring her back in another month."

Rebekah and her father walked several days to get back home. All of their neighbors joined them as they entered their village.

"Is she well?" they asked.

"Let us hear her talk," said one.

When the people found out that Rebekah still could not talk, they made it hard on Rebekah's parents.

"We told you the white doctor could not help her."

"Why don't you take her to the witch doctor? He will make her well," said another.

"No," replied Rebekah's father. "We believe only

in the Living God and He will take care of her."

A month passed by and Rebekah still could not talk. Once again Rebekah and her father walked several days back to see Dr. Birch. They were greeted warmly and asked to wait until the doctor could see them. One of the nurses went to the hospital which was located directly behind the clinic and got Dr. Birch.

"The nurse tells me that you still cannot talk, Rebekah," said Dr. Birch as she walked toward Rebekah. "Would you let me put you back to sleep and see if we can find the problem?"

Rebekah agreed although frightened.

"Don't be afraid," Dr. Birch said gently. "I will not hurt you."

They prayed together and Rebekah was put to sleep. Once again they tilted her head back and looked down her throat.

Carefully she pushed the vocal cords apart to lift out the thing that was blocking Rebekah's speech.

"There it is," she called as she pulled her instrument out. "It's a fish scale!"

It measured only five-eighths inch in its widest part.

When Rebekah woke up, she began talking as usual.

"Can I have the fish scale?" asked her father.

"Sure," agreed Dr. Birch handing him the scale.

"I must show my neighbors the evil spirit Rebekah had. I want them to see that God showed the white doctor and nurses what was wrong."

Rebekah and her father returned to their village. The people came from villages all around to see the scale and to hear about God.

Today Dr. Birch is working in a hospital in Columbus, Ohio. She loves to travel on her days off and tell people here in the States about God and the work of missions.

73

Chapter 16
God's Design for Larry

Larry asked Jesus into his heart during his third year of high school at the Houghton Academy. He had grown up hearing about Jesus. He knew that everyone should ask for their sins to be forgiven, but he just hadn't done it. He had memorized many Scripture verses and knew that he should be saved. Then one day, Jesus spoke in a special way to Larry's heart. Larry knew he had to pray. He made his way to the church and found a small room under the choir loft. There he accepted Jesus into his heart.

God's design for Larry was serving in the States as a heart specialist. Larry's father had always felt and said that becoming a doctor must be a wonderful calling. That way one could serve Jesus either in the States or overseas. Larry had watched his father study medical books and spend many hours treating the sick people in Sierra Leone. This touched his heart, and he began to dream about becoming a doctor.

The dream was interrupted during his second year of college. All young men were expected to enlist in the service. Larry was able to finish that year of college before joining the Navy. He passed a special test and was placed in a school to learn radio technology.

Larry had become good friends with a young lady, Roberta Chess, in college. They wrote each other faithfully while Larry was in the Navy and were later married.

Following his years of service, Larry went back to college and his dream of becoming a doctor. He was able to attend the University of Michigan Medical School as his mother had asked in prayer. The studies were hard and the hours stretched into years before he received his degree and became a heart specialist.

Today Larry is serving in Jacksonville, Florida. He has a private practice and works in a heart-catherization laboratory. The Larry Birches have four sons (Steven, Greggory, Richard and Robert) and three grandsons (Charles, Scott, and Christopher).

W. K. F. M. 1993

KINGSTON WESLEYAN
CHURCH LIBRARY